CRYPTO CURRENCY TRADING AND INVESTMENT:

A MANUAL TO BEGIN YOUR CRYPTO JOUNEY

BY

TOM OWENS

TOM OWENS

All rights reserved.

No part of this book may be reproduced, stored in any retrieval system or transmitted in any form or by any means of photocopying, electronic, mechanical, recording or otherwise without the permission of the author and publisher

Copyright©2023 Tom Owens Ph.D

Table of Contents

INTRODUCTION 5

SECTION ONE 6

WHAT IS CRPTO CURRENCY? 6

    Categorization of Crypto: Coins vs. Tokens 6

    What is an ICO? 7

    Understanding Crptocurrency 9

    List of Crpto Currencies and their Market Value 11

SECTION TWO 12

STAKING 12

WHAT IS STAKING IN CRYPTOCURRENCY? 12

    Different forms of staking 12

    Legal development of Crypto lending 13

    Financial market law Appraisal : Unauthorized staking 14

SECTION THREE 17

LENDING 17

    What Is Lending? 17

    What is lending in Crptocurrency 18

    Cash lending in crypto markets: the advantages 18

    The Marketplace 19

    Financing portals 21

SECTION FOUR 24

NFTS 24

What are NFTs? 24

Understanding NFTs 24

Literature Review 28

Non-Fungible Tokens (NFT): An innovation that presents an opportunity for everyone seeking to tap digital assets? 29

Why are NFTs so expensive? 30

How to take advantage of NFTs 30

SECTION FIVE 34

CRYPTOCURRENCY MINING 34

What Is Mining? 34

What is mining in Cryptocurrency? 34

Software: Bitcoin Mining Software for Windows 35

Hardware: Bitcoin Mining Software for Windows 37

SECTION SIX 38

AIRDROPS 38

Demystifying the Definition of an Airdrop: understanding What is it and How Does it Work? 38

CONCLUSION 41

TOM OWENS

INTRODUCTION

Cryptocurrency refers to the brand-new kind of money protected by encryption. The recent tendency has leaned heavily toward Cryptocurrencies, and this era has seen many of them. One of the most widely used Cryptocurrencies nowadays is Bitcoin, Ethereum, Litecoin, and many more are among the other currencies.

It's remarkable that so few business owners have realized the advantages of Cryptocurrencies. Like any sectors, there are dangers, but the potential for profit is far greater than in traditional finance. Although there is a lot of technical language used in the Cryptocurrency sector, many of the fundamental ideas are the same as those in traditional banking; they just go by new names. The names "Web3," "DeFi," "Cryptocurrency," and "Blockchain" might be regarded as basically the same thing. The Cryptocurrency market is still developing and has a long way to go. More individuals enter the business as the value of Crypto assets rises. These novices are always attempting to understand how to profit from Cryptocurrencies. But ultimately, the enduring ideas still hold true. Maintain your course and see your plans through to completion. Avoid grabbing hold of every chance you see since doing so will cause you to be divided among too many different initiatives.

Be selective with your investments and avoid taking on more than you can handle. Simple crypto staking gives excellent benefits even on its own. Due to excessive greed and bad investing psychology, many investors are still losing money on Web3. Across all markets, separating the wheat from the chaff is a crucial investment principle.

7

SECTION ONE

WHAT IS CRPTO CURRENCY?

Cryptocurrency is a type of digital money that functions independently of a central bank by using encryption algorithms and cryptographic methods to control the creation of units of currency and confirm the movement of cash. It performs the same purpose as a virtual medium, but Cryptocurrency owners may swap these digital assets without depending on a financial institution to handle each transaction, as opposed to hanging on to a physical piece of paper. Through the use of Blockchain technology and computer code, these transactions are processed and completed via a peer-to-peer network. Bitcoin, among other Cryptocurrencies, is built on the Blockchain technology. Blockchain technology was created for the first time in 2009 by an unidentified creator using the alias Satoshi Nakamoto.

"A tamper-evident, shared digital ledger that records transactions in a public or private peer-to-peer network," is what Blockchain is defined as. The ledger, which is distributed to all network participants, has a chronological chain of blocks with cryptographic hash links that permanently record the history of asset trades between network participants. The term "Blockchain" refers to a chain of connected and chained transaction blocks that are all confirmed and certified; this chain extends from the oldest block to the most recent block. Members of a Blockchain network may only examine transactions that are relevant to them, making the Blockchain a single source of truth. As a result, peer-to-peer transactions may now be carried out securely without the need for a middleman, like a bank, thanks to Blockchain technology.

Categorization of Crypto: Coins vs. Tokens

Coins are Cryptocurrencies that have their own independent, standalone Blockchain, whereas tokens can be any Cryptocurrency that is constructed on top of an already existing Blockchain.

To run and exist, tokens thus need to be hosted by another platform. Coins are used to hold value and make payments for goods and services in a manner similar to that of actual money, whereas tokens stand for digital assets with more functionality. Tokens may stand in for nearly any fungible and tradable item, including everything from commodities to voting rights. Tokens are more simpler to manufacture than coins since they simply need an established platform to function. Regular templates and smart contracts, which are programmable, self-executing computer codes. These tokens may be created and distributed to the public through what is known as an initial coin offering ("ICO"), though this is an apparent misnomer.

What is an ICO?

In the past few years, ICOs have gained enormous popularity as a way to finance online ventures. The most recent data shows that nearly $7 billion was raised in the United States alone through ICOs in 2018. The graph below shows that the United States really leads the world in the use of initial coin offerings (ICOs): Although the amount of money received through ICOs has increased significantly from the previous year, the quantity of ICOs seems to be falling in 2019. Companies seeking to fund their Cryptocurrency initiatives through methods complying with the securities regulations may be the cause of this huge decline. However, despite the downturn, some businesses continue to decide to raise money using ICOs. What is an ICO, then? "An ICO is a fundraising event that uses distributed ledger technology and offers participants a "token" or "coin" in exchange for cash (fiat money) or Cryptocurrencies like Ether or Bitcoin. The usage of a service that will be created and provided by the issuer is often one of the rights that a token's holders are entitled to. The ICO sponsors finance a venture or initiative using the money raised from the token sale. However, tokens sold in ICOs may also grant profit rights, may increase in value, and can be exchanged, much like stock securities. Tokens from initial coin offerings don't signify ownership in a business. The first-ever ICO occurred in 2013, ushering in an alternate form of financing for startup businesses. The ability for investors to profit from their digital asset instrument—typically by selling their tokens on the secondary market once value is produced and the digital project takes off—is another way that ICOs are comparable to traditional IPOs. A development team often launches an ICO using an internet channel, such a Cryptocurrency website or forum, to start the process. Access to the project's website, which will include the "white paper," an essential component of the ICO procedure, will probably, be included in this announcement. The project and important ICO terms will be covered in the white paper, includes subscription information, a schedule, the project's plan, how the funds will be spent, and the benefits of the initiative. Essentially all the data a potential investor would require to make their decision about whether or not to participate in the project. Because ICOs are frequently held before the project is in a profit-generating state, developers must concentrate on fostering investor confidence in their project in order to secure necessary funding. As a result, the white paper should provide important information to potential investors in a friendly manner. To inform potential investors, the development team also constructs a website and a group chat. These websites and group conversations offer information on progress and crucial, approaching dates. The development team will also provide a pre-sale, which is accessible for certain people who register for the "white list", Prior to the start of the ICO, the development team will also provide a pre-sale, which is only open to a select group of those who sign up for the "white list." Those with access can trade their currencies for the new tokens of the project at a discounted price during the pre-sale, which is conducted for a set amount of time. However, the tokens will be worthless until the project is officially published, and their value on secondary markets will only be speculative. Additionally, the token vanishes if the project's financing target is not met and the contributions are refunded. An investor may take part in a public sale after the pre-sale by sending money to the issuer in return for fresh tokens during the subscription process.. Unlike the pre-sale, the public sale is usually open longer and opens to all investors.

Many ICOs do acquire the cash they require to start their platforms, despite the possibility that projects may fall short of expectations. For instance, the creators of the EOS program generated approximately $4.1 billion in only the project's ICO in June 2017. Even while an ICO may provide the required funds for a project, there is no assurance that the initiative will be profitable after it has been launched. In fact, a research contends that within four months of initial token sales, more than half of ICO businesses collapse. There are enticing "advantages" of ICOs that can offset their costs despite the substantial chance of failure. Entrepreneurs may rapidly and easily raise money thanks to ICOs. Unlike traditional fundraising techniques, ICOs are mostly unregulated. Ideally, ICOs provide business owners and developers a sense of the price that consumers would be willing to pay for their goods or services. Additionally, ICOs provide global visibility, community development without geographical restrictions, and most importantly cheap cash rising.

Understanding Crptocurrency

Trading Bitcoin on a Cryptocurrency exchange like Coinbase or Kraken is far from the only method to earn money and become engaged in decentralized finance, and generating your own token is almost straightforward as a result. In reality, lack of understanding is frequently the primary obstacle preventing more customers from adopting these less traditional DeFi tactics and learning about alternatives to conventional banking that can produce better results and profits. The latest technology is available. People can use this right now, said Jake Brukhman, founder and CEO of Coinfund. He claims that "Blockchain technology represents a hyper-disruptive

TOM OWENS

transformation of the digital operating system to the entire globe, much like the advent of the internet itself. The wonderful thing is that everyone can take advantage of these chances if they are willing to put in the effort to learn. Yes, you can profit from Crypto currencies. The majority of crypto assets come with a high level of risk because of their inherent volatility, while some call for specific knowledge or skill.

SECTION TWO

STAKING

WHAT IS STAKING IN CRYPTOCURRENCY?

Staking Crypto currency is a method of making passive income on digital assets that investors intend to retain for an extended period of time. It's similar to an interest-bearing savings account in that when you stake your holdings, you get a share of the return on those assets over time. You put your Bitcoin holdings to work when you stake them. It's a component of DeFi that Tally Greenberg, head of business development at crypto hosting company all nodes, believes will gain widespread traction. "Staking has been around since 2012."It's not going away because it's an income-generating instrument, and the entire Cryptocurrency business is going to develop," she adds. "This is not your normal savings account, where the maximum might range from 0.5% to 1.5% if it's a high-yield savings account. In the instance of staking, you might earn anywhere from 5% to 15% in passive revenue every year." While your Bitcoin assets are staked, they are utilized to avoid Blockchain mistakes. Staking can be very complex and entail manually verifying transactions, but it can also be quite easy, since more prominent crypto exchanges provide consumer-friendly staking alternatives. The disadvantage of staking is that your assets are locked up, making it unable to trade those coins throughout the vesting time. This option is likewise limited to Cryptocurrencies that employ a proof of stake mechanism rather than a proof of work method. Staking is not permitted on Bitcoin, but it is permitted on Solana and Ethereum.

Different forms of staking

Staking can take several forms. In the most basic example, the owner of the crypto-assets and the operator of the technological infrastructure are the same individual. Legally more intriguing are circumstances in which the ownership of the crypto-assets and the technical operator of the network node are not the same person. A service provider can contractually structure staking to qualify as a deposit under banking legislation. This is the scenario if the holder transfers all of the Cryptocurrencies to the operator, producing simply a claim in the amount of the transferred Cryptocurrency and no right of Reparability. Some systems offer explicit functions for the holder to appoint a third party as operator ("nominated" or "delegated" staking). In this instance, the holder is not required to give the operator authority of disposal of the crypto-assets, but he or she remains vulnerable to slashing if the operator makes a mistake. The data accessible on the Blockchain in delegated staking already shows that the delegated service provider is operating on behalf of his customer. The question of whether the operator is staking in his own or the client's name, on the other hand, can only be answered on the basis of the current contractual relationship.

The minimum stake in staking is frequently substantial. It is Ether in the Ethereum system, and hence presently worth roughly CHF 100,000. As a result, joint or non-segregated staking is also available in practice ("pooled" staking). Although this alternative is the most rigorous legally, it is sometimes the most affordable.

Legal development of Crypto lending

Crypto-assets are frequently kept not by the beneficial owner, but by a matching service provider. Depending on how it is constructed, safeguarding by a depository can provide various benefits to crypto-asset holders, such as secure storage and administration of private keys or the easy exchange of crypto-assets for state currencies. Whether or whether the crypto-assets in question might have been divided on the basis of art in the case of the depository's insolvency, and the extent to which there was a gap to be closed is debatable in the literature and not resolved by case law. With the adoption of art, the legislature has removed this legal ambiguity. Clients of such service providers now have an express right to separation and hence a comparable legal standing under bankruptcy law as holders of items kept in custody under specific situations.

Financial market law Appraisal : Unauthorized staking

This describes the extent to which staking can be carried out without a license and the situations in which a fintech or even bank license is required

For the fintech license to be applicable, the licensee must not "invest" the deposits or public assets. This requirement is intended to enforce the banks' renunciation of lending business. Public deposits or assets of the clients must therefore be available on a permanent basis37 and may not be invested for proprietary transactions in the name and for the account of the fintech institution. Risks for the client must be largely excluded and public deposits must be available in liquid form as well as crypto-assets in the form in which they were accepted, so that they can be forwarded or refunded within a reasonable period of time in accordance with their intended purpose. In addition, the clients' public deposits or crypto-assets held in collective custody must be kept separate from the fintech institution's funds. Alternatively, these must at least be recorded in the fintech institution's books in such a way that they can be shown separately from its own funds at any time. In addition, such an investment must be held in the currency in which the client's claim for repayment is denominated. Lending business, which is prohibited under the fintech license, also constitutes a classic proprietary business of the bank, i.e. a business of the bank in its own name and for its own account. Conversely, in the case of fiduciary transactions, i.e. transactions in one's own name but for the account of the client, the long-standing practice of the SFBC (FINMA's predecessor authority) must be taken into account in order not to fall under the banking license requirement probably also within the 14 scope of the investment prohibition of the fintech license: It must therefore be stated illegally binding form vis-à-vis the client that the investment is made for the client's account, i.e. that all risks and therefore also the del credere and transfer risk are borne by the client. However, the relevant lending business for banking purposes is affirmed if client funds are pooled, i.e. held in collective custody, in order to make investments that do not correspond in currency and maturity to the obligations entered into vis-à-vis the clients, the investors are promised a minimum return or currency losses are assumed, and neither the details nor the type of investments made are evident from the client statements, which means that there can no longer be any fiduciary investments. Taking into account the materials on the DLT legislation and the old SFBC practice on fiduciary investments, investments or staking in one's own name but for the account of a third party would therefore probably have to be permissible under the fintech license and would not violate the investment prohibition, provided in particular that the type of crypto-asset is not changed and the client bears all risks. In this respect, the question arises as to whether slashing also represents a risk that must be borne by the client. In our opinion, slashing is an error in the validation process that is either hardware-related, software related or due to human error, i.e. an operational risk. If the corresponding nodes as well as the validation services are operated by the fintech institution itself, slashing would be an error within the fintech institution's sphere of influence, which would also constitute a breach of the fintech institution's duty to act diligently. This is not a classic risk due to third-party involvement, which the SFBC's practice requires to be transferred to the client, but an (operational) risk within the fintech company's sphere of influence, which should not even occur if the fintech company acts with caution. For these reasons, we believe it must be permissible for the fintech company to assume the slashing risk itself. In the case of a systematic promise of reimbursement to all staking clients in the event of slashing, the possible existence of an insurance transaction subject to authorization under the Insurance Supervision Act (ISA) must also be examined. Of the five criteria, the existence of insurance, i.e. (i) the existence of a risk or hazard, (ii) the payment of the insured (premium), (iii) the insurer's performance in the event of insurance/damage, (iv) the autonomy of the operation as

TOM OWENS

well as (v) the compensation of the risks according to the laws of statistics (scheduled business operation), at least criterion (iv) is unlikely to be met: The required independence of the organization serves to distinguish insurance from other legal transactions in which the obligation to provide a service in the event of a claim is merely an ancillary agreement or modality of the other party to the contract, whereby in this respect it is not the formal arrangement but the inner connection between the promised services that is decisive. In addition, as already mentioned, it could be argued that in those cases in which the wallet provider operates the node for staking himself, no slashing should occur due to the obligation to act diligently or that this would have to be taken over by the operator of the node if it should occur nonetheless, which ultimately means that there should never be a sector-typical transfer of risk to the client.

19

SECTION THREE

LENDING

What Is Lending?

Money lending is one of the primary engines of the contemporary economy. Debt has been considered as a crucial lubricant for commerce and investment since it was first utilized as a facilitator for trade thousands of years ago, and entire sectors today revolve around this exchange of current and future value. Hundreds of thousands of firms, services, and products have sprouted up over the years to make lending easier and safer, resulting in a complicated web of collateral and obligation with varied degrees of transparency. It was just a matter of time until the practice infiltrated the Cryptocurrency market.. As early as 2010, postings on the Bitcoin Talk1 forum talked about establishing "Bitcoin banks," and not long after, individuals began offering P2P lending services to earn a return on their holdings. Since then, the industry has developed to encompass a variety of enterprises, some of which are now well-established and many of which are just getting started, offering a variety of services covering a wide range of assets. Sector statistics suggest significant rise in demand for these services, which adds depth and complexity to an already complex subject. As we will see below, lending and borrowing in Bitcoin has several advantages. The introduction of Lending, however, can also add systemic risk, and could change the very nature of the underlying assets. Will the benefits outweigh the potential vulnerabilities? In this report, we aim to introduce the concept of crypto lending: who participates, as well as the advantages and risks of crypto lending. We also look at what the near future could hold for the service, and the impact this could have on the sector as a whole.

What is lending in Crptocurrency

Similar to staking, investors who have accumulated a large portfolio of Cryptocurrencies can lend those tokens, cash or stable coins to borrowers in exchange for interest payments. Unlike getting a loan from a bank, crypto lending is typically peer-to-peer lending and can be facilitated by a crypto lending platform. These advantages may lure new users and contribute to the ecosystem's overall growth.

This choice may include higher risks, as it is always conceivable that a borrower would default on his or her debt for the service, and the implications for the industry as a whole.

Cash lending in crypto markets: the advantages

Lending in the Cryptocurrency markets with crypto assets as collateral provides several benefits over lending in traditional markets for those who have extra income. But supply is still somewhat limited. Holders with surplus funds have a variety of other options for yielding returns at their disposal, including lending through conventional P2P platforms or investing in securities, both of which avoid the extra risk of requiring crypto assets as security. However, the unusual characteristics of crypto assets may wind up being one of the industry's selling factors for money lenders. In conventional P2P lending marketplaces, the borrower or a third party frequently holds the collateral on lien; the lender only assumes ownership if the borrower defaults, which might be a time-consuming and expensive procedure. However, asset collateral is frequently delivered straight to the lender in crypto lending. Because the assets are bearer, recovering them in the event of a default is not a problem, and the lender may rehypothecate the assets in the interim. Due to this, crypto-backed cash lending is more comparable to the repo market than the conventional asset-backed lending market. In the repo market, highly liquid assets are swapped for cash for a specified period of time at roughly 100% of face value.

The loan-to-value ratio is generally low, sometimes below 50%, which means that the lender receives a significantly larger portion of the value of the crypto asset than the cash given out money that the lender may utilize for other purposes. This is another allure for cash lenders. Additionally, the majority of Cryptocurrencies is more liquid than many other recognized forms of collateral, such real estate, and may be sold relatively easily should the loan-to-value ratio decline owing to market circumstances. Rewards are consistently credited; in actuality, slashing—for instance, as a result of a willful rule infringement or operational error is extremely uncommon.

If they so want, they can take part more once, increasing their payout in line with their initial investment. The myth that the staking reward is an interest rate for lending money to a third party is implied by this, On closer inspection, however, this comparison must be rejected since the invested money stays assigned to the holder in the system and is not transferred to a third party, even though it is blocked. Economically speaking, this transaction therefore does not include a loan but rather the use of a valuable as security. To be thorough, it should be mentioned that the stake in cutting is destroyed rather than realized, unlike typical collateral, such as that used to obtain a loan. Therefore, no third party acquires disposal authority over the blocked crypto-assets even in the event of cutting. However, in our opinion, whether or not the crypto-assets are used or destroyed in the case of cutting should not matter in the subsequent study. The deciding aspect is that they are only utilized as collateral and are not used by any other parties.

The Marketplace
Let's look at the service users before we talk about the loan platforms, the industry's "middlemen."

1) Crypto lenders: owners looking to receive a return on their Cryptocurrency holdings. These could be people or funds that are prepared to give up the flexibility of being able to exchange their assets in order to enhance any possible capital gain. Industry insiders claim that some investors just hold long positions in crypto assets for the yield, therefore hedging against a decline in price on the derivatives market.

2) Cash lenders: People with extra cash that are open to accepting Cryptocurrency as collateral. Comparing this to conventional cash lending has both benefits and drawbacks (see sidebar on following page). At the moment, stable coins, ether, and other Cryptocurrencies make up the majority of lending in the industry. However, as more owners seek to unleash the value of their crypto assets without selling them, demand for cash borrowing is rising. However, the availability of cash lenders is still very limited.

3) Cryptographic asset borrowers: these are typically people or businesses looking to trade or develop markets in digital assets. For instance, OTC desks may require borrowing in order to promptly fill a sizable purchase order, allowing them time to source the asset on the market without affecting the price. In order to start acquiring additional Crypto currency, a trader might need to deposit some Crypto currency on an exchange. Traders also often borrow to take advantage of arbitrage opportunities—executing a quick sale with borrowed assets is often more profitable than dashing into the market to buy before selling.

Selling short borrowed assets is an often mentioned purpose. A trader or investor who anticipates a decline in market value may borrow an asset, sell it on the open market, and then repurchase it at a reduced cost when it is time to make repayments. However, some industry insiders[2] assert that this sort of demand is less prevalent than anticipated because it is far simpler to capitalize on a gloomy outlook utilizing the futures markets.

4) Cash borrowers are owners of digital assets who want funding for investments or for their businesses' working capital. They may be people who need money but are worried about paying capital gains tax if they sell their assets, or they may be people who would prefer not to give up their possessions.

Brock Pierce, a contentious Bitcoin investor, used some of his assets last year to finance a mortgage on a house in Amsterdam. Cash borrowers may also include ICO issuers that need to obtain working capital to cover running costs but have a sizable quantity of ether or another Crypto currency in their treasury.

Financing portals

While there are many different business models, there are two main groups of crypto lending platforms: centralized, which are typically businesses that onboard customers selectively, manage payments, and custody assets; and decentralized, which are typically protocols that automate distributions and allocations.

1) Centralized: companies that, typically on a custodial basis, oversee the selective on boarding of users and the exchange of Crypto currency assets and cash. These might include: specialized companies like Genesis Capital, Unchained Capital, BlockFi, and Celsius (this list is not exhaustive); OTC desks that seek to optimize the efficiency of their Cryptocurrency positions while providing clients with simpler trading conditions; exchanges that use margin lending to draw users systems that consolidate margin trading opportunities across a number of exchanges, like Tagomi. Some sites, including Celsius and Nexo, have released tokens that provide holders benefits like discounts and income sharing. Loan information that originated at centralized platforms is not always readily available.

For the time being, all businesses remain private, and public disclosure is optional. One of the biggest lenders in the Cryptocurrency industry, Genesis Capital, releases a quarterly report4 with data that sheds some light on the development of the market. Their loan originations increased by 250% in Q3 of 2019; as a result, they have already loaned over $3 billion since March 2018.

2) Decentralized: protocols that automate the distribution of loans and interest payments by using smart contracts. These only deal in crypto assets, are often non-custodial, and send money straight to consumers' wallets. ETHLend, Maker, and Compound are a few examples. Some are integrated with decentralized trading systems, such as dYdX.

Individual traders drawn to these platforms by the returns and developers interested in experimenting with the technology are often the users. Since the transactions are recorded on open Blockchains, data for decentralized lending is more transparent than for centralized lending. LoanScan, DeFi Pulse, and DeFi Stats are three examples of data providers who concentrate on this subsector. 2019 saw the issuance of on-chain loans totaling more over $600 million, according to DeFi analytics platform LoanScan. Although full data for centralized platforms is difficult to get, combining the self-reported deposits data with the on-chain deposits data illustrates the sector's expansion over the last year. 2019 saw a sharp increase in DeFi loans, attracting Ethereum investors amid a bad market. Its appeal among investors who want to retain ether for a long time is indicated by this circular trend, which begs the issue of what DeFi initiatives must do to expand beyond this group of early adopters. The benefits of cash lending in Crypto currency marketplaces Lending in the Crypto currency markets with crypto assets as collateral provides several benefits over lending in conventional markets for those with surplus cash. But supply is still somewhat limited.

TOM OWENS

Holders with surplus funds have a variety of other options for yielding returns at their disposal, including lending through conventional P2P platforms or investing in securities, both of which avoid the extra risk of requiring crypto assets as security. However, the unusual characteristics of crypto assets may wind up being one of the industry's selling factors for money lenders. In conventional P2P lending marketplaces, the borrower or a third party frequently holds the collateral on lien; the lender only assumes ownership if the borrower defaults, which might be a time-consuming and expensive procedure. However, asset collateral is frequently delivered straight to the lender in crypto lending. Because the assets are bearer, recovering them in the event of a default is not a problem, and the lender may re-hypothecate the assets in the interim. Due to this, crypto-backed cash lending is more comparable to the repo market than the conventional asset-backed lending market. In the repo market, highly liquid assets are swapped for cash for a specified period of time at roughly 100% of face value.

The loan-to-value ratio is generally low, sometimes below 50%, which means that the lender receives a significantly larger portion of the value of the crypto asset than the cash given out—money that the lender may utilize for other purposes. This is another allure for cash lenders. Additionally, the majorities of Cryptocurrencies are more liquid than many other recognized forms of collateral, such real estate, and may be sold relatively easily should the loan-to-value ratio decline owing to market circumstances.

27

SECTION FOUR

NFTS

What are NFTs?

A digital certificate of ownership known as an NFT may be issued for any type of underlying asset. An NFT is a limited-edition digital asset that is one of a kind, giving holders a feeling of community, and should be utilized by creators, collectors, curators, conventional institutions, and culture custodians alike. To the uninformed, crypto may appear confusing and difficult to grasp. Unlike fungible tokens, which may be replaced, inertly modified, divided, or sold in pieces, non-fungible tokens (NFTs) cannot be done. Non-fungible.com lists the following six common NFT kinds and use cases:

- Sports i.e. NBA Topshot

- Gaming i.e. Plasma Bears

- Art i.e. ArtBlocks

- Utility i.e. Ethereum Name Service

- Metaverse i.e. Decentraland

- Collectibles i.e. CryptoPunks, BAYC, Afrodriods

Understanding NFTs

Non-Fungible Tokens are known as NFTs. But you might be thinking, what exactly is a token? I would also ponder. A Cryptocurrency token or token is a smart contract that may stand in for anything, including intangible items as well as tangible ones like your diamond jewelry and real estate. Tokens may or may not be fungible. Tradable assets produced on an established Blockchain, such as Ethereum, the most well-known token platform, such as your Doge coin are considered to be fungible tokens. Fungible tokens, such as the ERC-20 and BEP-20 tokens on

Ethereum and Bitcoin, respectively, may be traded in smaller quantities; for example, you can exchange 1 Bitcoin for another Bitcoin or 100,000,000 satoshis (units of Bitcoin), and the value will remain the same.

The reverse is true for NFTs, which are crypto tokens created using hashing techniques and connected to physical assets like real estate or digital assets like video clips, JPEGs, or PNGs using Blockchain technology. In contrast to fungible tokens, an NFT is considered to be unique due to its information, which acts as a digital "title deed" when an NFT is produced. Therefore, when an NFT, such as an ERC721 token on Ethereum's blockchain, is generated, it is not simply the digital asset but also the one and only ERC721 token—the "title deed" or artist's signature, which is the original—that adds value. When a digital asset is sold or purchased, a digital copy of the "original copy made/received by me" is created. This overcomes the problem of trackable provenance in the market by using Blockchain. In other words, the asset is a fake in all other forms.

NFTs, or non-fungible tokens, can be interactive digital artwork, video, music, or other forms of digital media. However, there is just one of them, and it is Ethereum-based. NFT collectors and makers can be people. By putting their digital creations on the Blockchain, creators may have access to a large audience of prospective customers throughout the world and potentially earn royalties as their work is exchanged. The ability to purchase digital art or other NFTs at a discount offers collectors the possibility to possibly profit from the work's value over time. According to Brukhman, "the typical person does not spend money on art." "With NFTs, that is drastically altering. There are emerging artists exhibiting their work, and the cost of collecting art has decreased. Marketplaces like OpenSea, Axie Marketplace, and Rarible provide NFTs for sale. People who buy NFTs or participate in any Cryptocurrency or DeFi activity online may become the target of fakes, frauds, or misleading information. Before starting, go with caution and conduct study. Although Cryptocurrencies and NFTs (non-fungible tokens) are traded on the same market, their prices have a less direct correlation over time. NFTs and Ethereum have a link; the price of NFTs has a direct impact on the price of Ethereum. New forms of payment, investment, and exchange have emerged as a result of technological progress, including Cryptocurrencies, non-fungible tokens (NFTs), which allow creators of digital material to profit from their labor, and FinTech-based financial goods and services. With the use of Blockchain technology, Cryptocurrency acts as a digital payment system where transactions aren't checked by banks. Blockchain technology has transformed organizational, economic, and environmental performance, revolutionizing the commercial world. Security, transparency, decentralization, peer-to-peer data synchronization, pseudo-anonymity or complete anonymity, and the veracity of the data are the major benefits of this technology. There are voices that solely highlight the drawbacks of this new technology, which they describe as "combining the worst elements of a Ponzi scheme, a soap bubble, and an ecological calamity." The newest digital phenomena, non-fungible tokens (NFT), uses Blockchain technology to confirm the ownership of particular assets, including music, photos, films, and pieces of virtual worlds. Digital artwork and other valuables become unique, verifiable assets thanks to NFTs: "NFTs are unique units of data recorded on a Blockchain or permanent ledger. The ownership of both physical and digital products is recorded using NFTs. Digital information may be created, arranged, used, and stored in an innovative manner that welcomes customers using NFTs. The introduction of the scarcity notion to the digital realm is the primary feature of NFTs. These digital tokens also present new opportunities for entrepreneurs to use Blockchain technology to transform the business environment.

NFTs are employed in a variety of industries, including sport, broadcasting, art, content production, and the tech-crypto industry. Other organizations, including museums or groups dedicated to animal protection, have also welcomed this invention. Given the negative externalities caused by human activities and the fast extinction of some animal and plant species, wildlife conservation is a major issue. The introduction of non-fungible crypto wildlife tokens is a way to finance this fundamental process that must be carried out in the unfulfilled term. In this sense, Blockchain technology may assist both the natural world and the tourism sector. In the area of intellectual property, NFTs may also be used more widely. Using Blockchain technology, it is possible to track changes in patent ownership in this industry. NFTs would also increase the market's liquidity and the potential for other organizations, such universities or R&D firms, to commercialize their discoveries. This paper's primary goal is to determine whether there is a relationship between Cryptocurrencies and the price of NFT over time. The study's findings will be helpful for Cryptocurrency and NFT issuers as well as for investors on the financial market who regularly restructure their portfolios and use these new assets for speculative or hedging purposes based on Blockchain technology. The research question that follows is, "Is there a causal link between the NFT price and the prices of Cryptocurrencies?"

The article is structured as follows to reply to the research question: The results of recent research on NFTs and Cryptocurrencies are discussed in the next section; The third component of the article contains the information and techniques used to test the research hypotheses. The fourth section of the paper summarizes the findings of the empirical analysis, and the concluding sections of the paper contain the closing remarks and conclusions.

Literature Review

The ability to monetize digital content from many assets and introduce scarcity into this complicated environment makes NFTs the next digital stars. NFTs advertise and profit from digital assets. NFTs are relatively new phenomena in technology that resembles the most well-known ones, such as Blockchain (2009) and smart contracts (2015). Following the huge success of Crypto Kitties, which began in late 2017 [36], their popularity has increased significantly. A game called Crypto Kitties allows players to purchase, trade, or amass digital kittens. The NFTs sector had a boom in 2021, and as Bitcoin transactions become more frequent, more customers are becoming interested in this market. Considering the decline in securities prices as a result of the COVID-19 crisis, the markets for NFTs and Cryptocurrencies are considered as alternatives to traditional financial markets. Additionally, similar to any new technology, there is some hesitancy on the part of both the businesses interested in advertising these assets and customers. which sophisticated explanations based on certain theories or models, such as the Technology Acceptance Model, Unified Theory of Acceptance and Use of Technology Model, are provided in the specialist literature.

NFT demand is growing, but it is unstable because of the unknowns and future advantages. The three key considerations for managers and business owners who are interested in NFTs are security, storage, and environmental sustainability (taking into account the energy that must be consumed for Blockchain mining). Scholars have called attention to the harmful externalities that Cryptocurrencies and NFTs have on the ecosystem because of the mining features. The success of NFT is a result of some of them including smart contracts that provide the original developers money based on subsequent transactions. NFTs are used in a wide range of industries. The use of NFT in the world of sports includes things like digital collectibles, tickets, monetizing athletes' reputations, transferable memberships, and ownership interests. Companies have grown more interested in these digital assets that may be leveraged to create sales channels and business models as NFT transactions have escalated. The market has become more consistent over time, and experts are now even referring to an ecosystem that includes various stakeholder types with distinct roles, including individual content creators, content owners, intermediaries (technical entities that oversee the development, security, etc.), and consumers. customers, collectors, investors, and speculators) as well as the development and upkeep of the NFT infrastructure; fintech marketplace firms. The majority of the studies that have been found focus on how NFTs might be used in various industries, emphasizing their potential for business reconfiguration and the ways that sports clubs and museums can sell goods and services. A research by Baker et al. examined the employment of NFTs in the American sports industry while taking into account the efforts made by various organizations to investigate potential future innovation prospects. The ability to trace and confirm the validity or ownership of digital assets is the major benefit provided by NFTs. Managers and businesspeople in this industry can control the sports market in new ways by pushing NFTs, taking into account the propensity of younger generations to utilize digital products. Blockchain technology is therefore viewed as a new way to reshape innovation, financial markets, and entrepreneurship as well as to create new ecosystems. However, some voices have also called attention to the use of Cryptocurrencies and NFTs for money laundering and tax evasion by businesspeople and celebrities in the entertainment industry.

Non-Fungible Tokens (NFT): An innovation that presents an opportunity for everyone seeking to tap digital assets?

As previously noted NFTs provide a fantastic investment opportunity and have a wide range of applications. Despite the fact that owners frequently advertise it as a status symbol by disclosing a purchase and posting NFTs as profile images on social media, it actually stands for more.

Due to the availability of digital platforms to mint, sell, price, and bid for NFTs, they are time and cost efficient with less headache associated with valuation. A phony NFT cannot be sold due of its traceable origin and provable historical evidence. NFTs may be verified online since ownership data are updated on Blockchain as soon as the artwork is minted, purchased, and sold again. Also, opportunities for fractional ownership offer buyers an opportunity for diversification.

Why are NFTs so expensive?
for the same reason that a painting at, let's say, a Sotheby's auction, is pricey in the actual world. I am aware that the scope of this response is limited to NFTs that are pieces of art or collectibles, and I can already feel your side-eye, just like Steph Curry's BAYC NFT. You are concerned about how pricey NFTs are. NFTs are costly for simple yet complicated reasons. Although you and I can download a photograph of the Mona Lisa from Google, do we actually possess the original painting? Basically, no. As a result, just like any other asset in the real world, the price of NFTs depends on how much buyers are ready to give up in exchange for the asset. Additionally, the only valuable NFTs are the original ones that have the artist's signature, metadata, or a title deed. That is, the NFT image above is worth zero, because only the holder – Steph Curry has the original, with the unique metadata.

How to take advantage of NFTs
Institutions, collectors, and producers can all benefit from NFTs in different ways. Institutions. NFTs can be purchased by corporations as a saleable asset. Corporate can develop NFTs for intriguing initiatives in the digital sphere and provide users with a portion of ownership. NFTs will also be very helpful for Web 3.0 initiatives for corporations. Collectors have the option to purchase, hold, or invest speculatively in NFTs via spread betting.

Here are six methods that inventors and conventional organizations can purchase NFTs, despite the fact that there are several application cases.

1. Traditional organizations like the Warri Kingdom can sell virtual lands or real estate within the kingdom to eager customers since they are virtual real estates.

2. Traditional institutions can produce virtual replicas of several essential events during a coronation, such as the King being crowned or a crucial speech, etc.

3. Traditional institutions can produce a digital representation of the king's crown, traditional clothing, sculptures, or what Yoruba speakers refer to as "shigidi," Benin bronzes, images of ancient monarchs, etc. as souvenirs or keepsakes.

4. Actors from well-known films, such as Chief Omego in Living in Bondage and Laburu in King of Boys, can be rendered in 3D as digital photographs.

5. Using sympathetic figures like Odenigbo, Olanna, and Kainene from Half a Yellow Sun as virtual representations or 3D renders, authors may bring major characters to life.

So, what next?

Collaboration is the secret to producing, minting, and selling NFTs profitably. Individual producers and collectors may be able to negotiate this more simply, but corporations may find it challenging and will thus need expertise.

Platforms like Rarible and Open Sea are good options for developers who want to produce and market NFTs. Check out Mintable if you want to mint for free without having to pay for gas.

Finally, as a final suggestion for readers who do not work as artists and have no ties to established institutions, I will leave you with this advice from a friend: "If your child enjoys drawing or painting, you should think about turning all of their creations into NFTs." Then give them a wallet for a Metamask. You retain memories, or perhaps as they grow older someone will pay millions for their foolish childhood artwork. More details about this are available here.

The Blockchain market is marked by unpredictability and volatility, with NFTs and other Cryptocurrencies experiencing extremely high risk. In this context, in order to contribute to the growing literature on the latter, our article examined the link between the price of Cryptocurrencies and the price of NFT. According to Dowling's hypotheses, we discovered that the prices of Bitcoin, Crypto Coins, and Ethereum all have an impact on the price of the NFT; however the NFT price only has a causal impact on the price of Ethereum. As a result, the price of Cryptocurrencies influences the price of NFT. This makes sense given that Cryptocurrencies are frequently used to acquire and sell NFTs. Lower purchasing power as a result of a decline in the value of Cryptocurrencies drags down the NFT market. Investors look for alternate investment options, such as those using ETH, the typical NFT denomination, in the event that Cryptocurrencies grow. Our findings show that the NFT market is vulnerable to shocks and volatile due to Cryptocurrencies. Even though the NFT market is more developed than the other Cryptocurrency markets, the NFTs price is determined by the prices of Cryptocurrencies, not the other way around, with the exception of the Ethereum price. These findings add to the body of knowledge on the consequences of spillover between different-sized Blockchain-based markets. Given the minimal connection between the price evolution of traditional assets and NFTs, these results are advantageous not only for investors in the emerging Cryptocurrency and NFTs markets but also for investors in existing financial markets who may diversify their portfolios. As Cryptocurrencies demand significant risk-mitigation avenues for investors and financial markets, this study may also assist policymakers and regulators in structuring and improving their policies toward participating in financial markets. Therefore, our findings produce insightful conclusions and policy implications that emphasize the advantages of investing in Blockchain markets and offer solutions to minimize their hazards.

The analysis time as well as the variables included was some of the research's limitations, which the authors are aware of. In order to determine the significance of economic uncertainty in these market sectors, future research may focus on the returns of NFTs and Cryptocurrencies for the pre-pandemic era and the pandemic period. The examination of the speculative and hedging opportunities that these assets give to portfolio investors in various markets should also be taken into account by authors, especially in light of the appeal of Cryptocurrencies for investors, particularly during the epidemic era (European, American, and Asian markets). Analysis of the relationships between the markets for conventional assets like gold or oil and cryptocurrencies can be another future direction of research.

SECTION FIVE

CRYPTOCURRENCY MINING

What Is Mining?

Mining is the process of drawing, obtaining, or obtaining anything useful from a pile. Since the discovery of the valuable metals in the earth's core, we have a solid understanding of the mining idea. The most valuable materials we can mine are gold, silver, copper, salt, iron, oil, and many others. There has never been a method for mining. To extract something of immense worth from a mass of meaningless items calls for a constant, exhausting effort.

Mining is the name for this laborious endeavor and activity. If we wish to locate gold or any other precious metal, we may need to delve far below the surface of the earth. The result might be successful or unsuccessful at times. If the conclusion is unsuccessful, we must dig anew and go through the entire procedure again until we locate the mine containing the valuable metal and extract it from it.

What is mining in Cryptocurrency?

The broad definition of Cryptocurrency mining is the extraction of Crypt currency. Traditional mining and Cryptocurrency mining are not the same thing. By resolving difficult mathematical equations and problems, Bitcoin mining is done to get Cryptocurrency units. There is no central regulating body for the Cryptocurrency. As a result, there are only so many units of the coin.

Each unit contains a unique digital data and key that can only be discovered by doing an enormous number of computations. It must be accompanied by a cryptographic hash that satisfies specific criteria in order to correctly produce a block. Simply compute as many as you can and wait until you receive a hash that matches the required requirements is the only practical approach. A new block is created when the correct hash is discovered, and the miner who discovered it is rewarded with Bitcoin units.

Software: Bitcoin Mining Software for Windows
Bitcoin Miner

You can use Bitcoin Miner on Windows 10 and Windows 8.1. It offers a user-friendly UI, a power-saving mode, support for mining pools, and a quick share filing process. Profit reports are a helpful tool since they let you know whether or not your mining is lucrative. This program's most recent version is Bitcoin Miner 1.27.0.

BTCMiner

For ZTEX USB-FPGA modules 1.5, there is an Open Source Bitcoin miner called BTCMiner. These are some of the characteristics that BTCMiner has:

• Dynamic frequency scaling, whereby BTCMiner always selects the frequency with the largest percentage of valid hashes

• Ready-to-use Bitstream, requiring neither Xilinx software nor a license.

Additionally, it includes FPGA boards that may be utilized, each of which has a USB interface for programming and communication.

CGMiner

Among Bitcoin miners, CGMiner is likely the most well-known and popular program. CGMiner is based on the original code of CPU Miner. This software has many features but the main ones include:

- fan speed control

- remote interface capabilities

- self-detection of new blocks with a mini database

- multi GPU support

- CPU mining support

BFGMiner

BFGMiner and CGMiner are nearly identical. The only significant distinction is that, unlike CGMiner, it is tailored for ASICs rather than GPUs. Mining with free Mesa/LLVM OpenCL, reordering ADL devices by PCI bus ID, integrated over clocking, and fan management are just a few of the special features of BFGMiner.

EasyMiner

EasyMiner is a GUI-based tool that serves as a handy wrapper for the CGMiner and BFGMiner programs. Both the stratum mining protocol and the getwork mining protocol are supported by this program. Additionally, it may be utilized for both solo and group mining. Its primary functions include setting up your miner and offering performance graphs for simple visualization of your mining activities.

Bitcoin Mining Software for Linux

CGMiner

Currently, CGMiner is likely the most well-known and widely used Bitcoin mining software. CGMiner is built using the original CPU Miner source code. Fan speed control, remote interface capabilities, self-detection of new blocks with a tiny database, multi GPU support, and CPU mining support are some of the primary features of this program.

BFGMiner

This is nearly identical to CGMiner. The only significant distinction is that, unlike CGMiner, it is tailored for ASICs rather than GPUs. Mining with free Mesa/LLVM OpenCL, reordering ADL devices by PCI bus ID, integrated over clocking, and fan management are just a few of the special features of BFGMiner.

EasyMiner

EasyMiner is a GUI-based program that serves as a handy wrapper for the CGMiner and BFGMiner programs. Both the stratum mining protocol and the network mining protocol are supported by this program. Additionally, it may be utilized for both solo and group mining.

Its primary functions include setting up your miner and offering performance graphs for simple visualization of your mining activities.

Bitcoin mining application for Mac OS X

RPC Miner

RPC Miner integrates with Mac OS APIs and systems and may be used with Mac OS 10.6 or later.

Hardware: Bitcoin Mining Software for Windows

What kind of equipment is used to mine cryptocurrencies?

There isn't a particular piece of hardware for cryptocurrencies; sometimes the GPU, other times the CPU. It totally depends on the miners' study.

SECTION SIX

AIRDROPS

Demystifying the Definition of an Airdrop: Understanding what is it and how it Does Work

In laymen's terms an airdrop is the practice through which developers of a new Cryptocurrency-based project distribute "free" tokens to community members (also known as "users"). Why do developers give out tokens for "free"? An airdrop may be used as a distribution method as well as a marketing strategy. It is essential for developers to successfully market their new products given that there are already more than 1,900 Cryptocurrencies available. New methods of generating awareness have emerged as a result of increased competition in a crowded market. Crypto businesses are employing airdrops as a marketing alternative to ICO advertising, which is currently prohibited by many web platforms (including Facebook). Airdropping, when carried out ethically, may be a successful marketing strategy to launch a new initiative. Airdrops are utilized for both "popular" tokens and "obscure" tokens, not just the former the airdrop of TRX tokens worth $1.7 million by the Tron Foundation to community members who owned Ethereum was completed in May 2018. Tron is a well-known Cryptocurrency with a market valuation of over $3.8 billion, making it one of the most valuable ones available attempting to generate "buzz" by airdropping their tokens. Developers therefore rely on both consumers and these distributions to generate talk about their brands. Despite the fact that these airdropped tokens are advertised as "free," receivers must eventually pay for them. The initiative's creators believe that the recipient of the airdrop will take activities that will advance the project i.e., offering marketing assistance in return for tokens. Despite the claim that they are "free," airdrops sometimes require the completion of quick tasks, such as posting to social media sites, writing a blog, or even contacting a specific member of the Blockchain project. In essence, this acts as a "lead generating and referral campaign," handing over the promotion to the locals. Additionally, these free token offers are meant to reward early investors who have already made investments by giving them more tokens. Companies believe that by using these strategies, early investors would continue to hold onto their tokens. These huge token drops serve as both a distribution tool and a token drop. To distribute tokens to the general public, airdrops may take place concurrently with or after an initial coin offering (ICO). Developers may use a free token giveaway as a way to jump start long-term network growth after money is raised for the project through token sales (ICO). Mass adoption of the token is, of course, the ultimate goal.

Project creators create a community for their token by paying users with these "freebies." Despite the fact that users only receive modest quantities of tokens, the viewership is often sizable. As a result, a community of token holders and users is effectively created. This "community formation" raises awareness, which might increase demand for the token. This is due to the inevitable possibility that some users who receive the "free" tokens may conduct more study and elect to buy more tokens. Additionally, users frequently place a higher value on a token they currently possess than one they acquire from the open market. As a result, this "endowment effect" encourages users to expand the token's network and community. The ability to "test, trade, and deal with unknown crypto assets without having to mine or invest first" is an advantage for users who receive "free" tokens. Prior to distribution, an airdrop may be unannounced or disclosed. Users are pleasantly delighted when they discover fresh tokens in their digital wallets during an unscheduled airdrop. In some cases, users must have a specific cryptocurrency or a specified quantity of crypto tokens in their wallets in order for the distribution to occur. After taking a "snapshot" of a block of a certain Cryptocurrency, developers may choose to distribute tokens, giving holders of that currency rights. to "free" tokens (as of the snapshot date). Users can visit websites that list scheduled airdrops in the case of publicized airdrops and subscribe to the airdrops of their choosing. Although many detractors consider these "free" releases to be a complete waste of time, developers find airdrops to be an attractive low-cost marketing approach. The supply of tokens might be diluted if too many are distributed. Furthermore, there is no assurance that the tokens would be kept by their receivers. The token's value will probably decline if enough recipients sell it after getting it. If there are enough sales, the token can disappear. Furthermore, developers frequently have unrealistic expectations Users holding on to airdropped tokens alone does not guarantee an increase in the token's use. Furthermore, it does not imply that users do not consider the tokens to be spam. Without enough incentives, token owners will stop utilizing the product, which would prevent the network from expanding.

Each holder is really more likely to profit from the network's expansion than to advertise or utilize it directly. Due to the limited supply of tokens and the fact that these speculative users are hoarding them instead of using them, they may potentially have a detrimental effect on the network. Because receivers are driven by the promise of "free" money and lack genuine incentives to utilize the product, enhance its usefulness, or expand the network, opponents of airdrops see the distributions as "flawed." However, for some businesses, the advantages outweigh the drawbacks of doing a "free" token giveaway.

CONCLUSION

One of the ways to generate money with Cryptocurrency is by trading different Cryptocurrencies. Despite having a daily average volume of trades that is just 1% of the foreign exchange market, the Cryptocurrency market is very volatile. Therefore, it is possible to engage in short-term trading. The Cryptocurrency sector has a lot of room to develop even if it is now rather tiny. Similar to how there are several cryptos purchasing sites like Binance, Coinbase, and Robinhood, there are many ways to profit from Cryptocurrencies.

Essentially, there are quite a few methods for you to make legitimate money with Cryptocurrencies, other than the obvious way of trading which has been given in this work.

www.ingramcontent.com/pod-product-compliance
Lightning Source LLC
Chambersburg PA
CBHW050316220526
45465CB00005B/2015